All About Love

Poems by

Susan Lidia Montes De Aragon

A publication of

Eber & Wein Publishing

Pennsylvania

All About Love
Copyright © 2022 by Susan Lidia Montes De Aragon

All rights reserved under the International and Pan-American copyright conventions. No part of this book may be reproduced, stored in a retrieval system, or transmitted in any form, electronic, mechanical, or by other means, without written permission of the author.

Library of Congress
Cataloging in Publication Data

ISBN 978-1-60880-714-7

Proudly manufactured in the United States of America by

Eber & Wein Publishing
Pennsylvania

Of all emotions, love is the one that constantly drives our lives. Love can take our hearts, full of happiness, high into Heaven; or drown us in a sea of sadness.

We are always dreaming to find a perfect "soul mate" in the constant quest for love. God knows whether he is going to give us the opportunity in this short span on life.

These poems reflect my desire to fill that empty space in my heart with the sincere love of someone that understands and cares for me. What is life without love or the companionship of someone that understands us?...

And, after all the emotional struggle, I found my quest for love to be an exciting and fulfilling adventure no matter what the ending came to be. Because, at the end, there is always something to gain: even if it is a minute, infinite moment of beautiful love and passion. It is always good to enjoy, to the fullest, every adoring moment.

All About Love

Contents

The Quest for Love	1
You Did Not Know	2
The Waiting	3
If	4
Invisible Love	5
A Superficial Touch	6
To David	7
A Loving Rose	8
No Romance	9
To Feel Alive	10
Goodbye	11
To Patriccio	12
An Empty Doll	13
You	14
That Smile	15
Ron	16
Don't Enslave My Soul	17
Love Quest	18
To John	19
To Bill	20
He	21
To Peter	22
Doubts	23
To Peter	24
No Connection	25
Fred	26
To Ron	27
A Need	28
A Trace of You	29

Don't Go	30
To Howard	31
The Walk	32
To My Friend from India	33
To Birch	34
Sadness	35
Another Plan	36
The Man Doesn't Love Me	37
Do I Look Like Her?...	38
To Howard	39
To Mr. Goodman	40
Poor Heart	41
Terry	42
Frustration	43
Without Love	44
The Quiet Look	45
To Eddie	46
Goodbye	47
Michael	48
Eddie	49
Pure Delight	50
I Should of Known	51
Ring of Fire	52
The Last Word	53
Betrayal	55
Don't Talk to Me	56
In the Cold	57
Puzzled	58
Lust	59
Why?...	60
To Fernando	61
Planting a Seed	62
He Doesn't Care for Me	63
To Larry	64
To Michael	65
To Jack	66

Sparks of Dreams That Have Not Died	67
To Peter	68
Sam	69
Your Charming Smile	70
Prayer for Love	71
Hi Emptiness	72
A Tender Moment	73
Without Love	74
To Charles	75
Fade Away…	76
Thanks!...	77
To My One and Only	79

The Quest for Love

Oh love... love...
When are you going to come?
I almost don't believe in love
Because there is no love of mine...

Oh birds... birds...
When are you going to teach me to fly?...
I almost think I'm going to fall
In arms of darkness, where there is no light...

And when the night is coming fast
The lips of sweet remembrances my soul touch.
The arms of a gentle heart to hold me tied,
In loving me, to dream with one...

To touch your hands and feeling mine,
To see your eyes and going far,
To touch your lips, to touch your heart,
And hear a voice, but it's a sound...

And still the night is passing sweet;
When it is white it's only dreams.
To hear the words of a lover's heart
Murmuring tenderly because of love...

Susan Lidia Montes De Aragon

You Did Not Know

You did not know, hidden in the corners
Of my heart,
Opening like a flower bud,
Damp in morning dew,
My love for you...

You did not perceive
The sparkles in my eyes
When you arrived,
And talked to me...

You did not know
Because you did not feel
The tenderness of my smile,
The passion when our lips met,
The softness of my touch,
The pounding of my heart
When dancing close to you...

And you ignored
The pain reflected in my face
When you passed by
And walked away
To meet another...

The Waiting

I'm still waiting for you, love of my life;
Whose face is still hiding among the shadows of my dreams.
If you could know the anguish of my heart
Because my arms cannot hold you, near to me...
Many buds of flowers, illusions of my soul, had dried
Before the breath of spring had made bloom;
And, with them, my newest dreams of tenderness had died...
And I miss living my love, the love I need.
There is so much for you waiting, within...
Oh come, come close, to touch my waiting hands
With loving lips, love of my dreams...

Susan Lidia Montes De Aragon

If

*If you are able to embrace with your eyes my lonely soul,
And with your words cut my heart
With the sweetest sword,
I'll be yours.*

*If you are able to see me free of body;
Floating as I am, and love me;
And if you are yearning every night to drink only from
my cup,
I will take your love and only yours be.*

*If you flourish with my laughter,
And fall in despair with my tears.
If you would be just one of my loving dreams,
An illusion of youth already lost.*

*Nobody could change a touch of your lips
For a thousand ships filled with gold,
And yes, oh yes,
I'll be yours...*

All About Love

Invisible Love

*There is a hole in my heart
That awaits to be filled with your love,
My hands, extended,
Are yearning for the warmth of your loving touch…*

*My lips were sealed with empty kisses of lovers
I had,
Who only offered me passion,
And filled me with foolish, romantic dreams that,
broken, died.*

*I feel like a little cotton seed,
Floating softly at the mercy of the playful wind,
Waiting to fall into the bed of the land
To finally grow, its roots set free…*

*I feel like a lost, little butterfly,
Moving rapidly her wings in her searching flight
For the soothing, sweet nectar of every flower
Of colorful, green plants…*

*Where can I find you
To stay and share this short road of my life?…
Am I going to meet you before my last breath
Darkens this flame that my hope lights?…*

Susan Lidia Montes De Aragon

A Superficial Touch

I found myself with a little time
To think of you, of moments that passed,
To dig within my clouded mind,
And find a light within my heart...

Little I know of "you," except
Of things you said in casual talk.
Meanwhile, you told me "little lies,"
"The same as the other men I met," I thought...

You tried to impress me
Talking about experiences of sexual lust,
Like if the most important treasures
Is the empty pleasure of superficial touch...

You showed me pictures of many women,
You told me of many more.
I didn't care to listen about past "experiences."
My heart listening, closed its doors...

Oh, what are you looking for?...
One more picture to add to your collection?
Someone to touch in lust and pleasure
To keep in mind until tomorrow's recollection?...

And, engulfed in deceiving nightly shadows,
Between kisses of passion and tender embraces,
I'm giving in slowly and your desires following,
Moved by my own needs for your manly and illusive
protection...

All About Love

To David

Who is the one that brings me light
Among the shadows of my night
And, with beautiful words,
Delights my heart?...

Who is the one who brightens
My life with his smile
And brings me warmth,
When holding hands,
Meanwhile, together, we dance...

That's only you, Dave,
Who comes and goes
And never stays.
But brings me joy
In every way.

Will we ever get together?...
(Maybe some day).
What do you say?...

Susan Lidia Montes De Aragon

A Loving Rose

When I'm in love,
I feel sad and rejoice
With every mood he has.
Because I like to feel him very close
With every deep pounding of my heart...

Because I'm in love,
I'm cheering all the happy happenings
Crossing his life,
And, with a kiss, I like to wipe the tears
Brought by each sadness passing by...

I like to please him
And make true every wish
Crossing his mind.
I like to know him deeply,
To bring him closer and closer to my path...

Because when you're in love,
You give your soul to him
To carry gently in his hand.
You surrender to the protective
Embracing of his arms...

And sweetly place a loving rose
In the tender chambers of his heart
To carry always in his mind and soul
Until the end of time...

No Romance

I don't understand what drives my mind
To think of you...
You certainly did not try
To tell me sweet words and moved
My heart...
You even told me
You want adventure... but not romance...
Then, why do I think of you?...
If you are putting always aside
All feelings that for me are good...

You want with me a friendship that will last.
A friend more, in my large group,
And I don't mind.
But... my heart was confused
For being ignored as you passed by,
And calmly smile throwing a look
That is engraved deep in my mind,
And returns to delight me in my dreams
Until I am awake... and realized
There is no reason for what I feel.
In you "love" I will not find,
"Romance" is not your wish,
And I have to turn this page in the journey of my life...

Susan Lidia Montes De Aragon

To Feel Alive

I nourished my lonely heart as I laid down
To place my mind to rest.
The tender glimpse from your manly eyes
Stamped there ...

I desire to feel again the warmth of your lips
Touching my lips like when
I almost surrendered to our arms,
And in sweet delight felt...

The chapter of my book of life is almost closed.
I crave for those wonderful, romantic moments
In order to feel alive, before the beat of my heart is gone.
Because "love" is food to my soul before its rest...

All About Love

Goodbye

Like birds flying in the horizon,
I experienced, like a feather touching my heart,
The tenderness of love and fury of passion in which life falls;
And, in one of the rounds in the waltz of my heart,
I met you, the new man, "Don"...

Don: You came to me like the forceful winds
Pushing their way through the peaceful night,
And induced my heart to pound and stretch
To all the manly wishes and desires of your heart...

You hold material things, and superficial beauty,
Important in your mind,
And forget the beauty within everyone,
To push it away, to push it aside.

Meanwhile my soul lies, lonely and sad,
Until it's the next time to brake our empty embrace
And say to this meaningless passion goodbye...

Susan Lidia Montes De Aragon

To Patriccio

I don't want to recollect my foolish mistake,
Clutter my mind with thoughts of deeds
That already passed and I cannot change.
I only acted out of impulse because I'm sincere;
I was testing both of us, without any shame.
You seemed distant, impersonal, someone who does not feel.
YOU shattered my pride, bringing to my romantic soul a vague pain...
We are different... although our roots are the same.
YOU don't want ME to be close to you.
Last night, you were disrespectful, inconsiderate and rude.
(I could not understand what your goal was with me.)
Your arrogance and lack of care did not place me in the mood
To satisfy your craze for lust and in loving satisfaction BE...
Oh please, don't touch my poor heart,
Because, while my soul is looking for an adoring love,
You are only trying to purchase passion and lust.
Your intelligence, success, has attracted my attention,
But you don't want to meet my soul now or any other night;
Nor talked or even think of any affection;
That's just like telling my dreams of love goodbye
And, like a robot, BE without a heart and any normal expectations...

An Empty Doll

And I wonder what you think of me
After that crazy impulse that pushed me falling into
your arms again.
What spark of energy guided my thoughtless steps to be
An easy target of meaningless desires in your manly
game...

You probably think I'm an empty doll
With a desperate desire to be love—but no heart and
mind at all.
Because, even though I expect your attention,
Only indifference for me you showed.

And when you came, with me you danced.
And then, again, I was yours...
What a fool... it's only this desperate, burning desire
For you to light that little flame that warms my heart
That slowly drives me, step by step, to your side.

(To fall like a drying flower
To every wish of your mind...)

Susan Lidia Montes De Aragon

You

In the turmoil of my life,
Searching for peace, a moment's rest,
Many souls, parading, crossed my path,
But, I stopped a moment with you, to stay,
And you offered the sparkle of your smile,
The closeness and warmth of your embrace...

You traced pictures of all your future plans;
Empty pages to be filled, old ones to erase.
These are your tomorrow's dreams,
Some, sad nightmares to forget...

You want me falling into your passion,
Trapped, like flies in a spider web.
But, did you forget the bleeding of my heart
Because I will not hear your tender words, someday?...

What is hidden within the corner of your heart?...
Are you really the man
To offer me the profound, true offering of your love?...
Or will you leave the hands of fate to move you away...

That Smile

What happened to that smile that took my heart away?
It seemed to disappear as time went by,
Hiding in the pensive expression of your face,
My soul secretly waiting for a sign of love,
Nourished by the tenderness of your nightly embrace...
You lighted in me a torch of passion to satisfy your desires
In your manly quest.
I was hoping to come close to warm your heart,
And bath my soul with your imagined adoring jest...
And my eyes keep searching for the soft affection of that smile,
Before your indifference quiets completely the calls of my heart for what it craves...
Look at my eyes, hold me, tell me;
Don't ignore any more my lonely heart that needs to be held
Before the torch dies out... and it needs to leave...
Leaving behind a fragile silhouette printed in your bed...

Susan Lidia Montes De Aragon

Ron

"I'll be with you this time," he said,
"But I'll like you to know I have another.
She's the one that is in my heart.
I want you to be, what's left, my lover..."

"I'll dine with you, I'll kiss your lips,
I'll dance a song—but don't you bother
To touch my soul with your foolish dreams.
For you, my dear, I'll be your lover..."

"I'll look at your eyes, I'll hold your hands,
I'll be to you a confidant, a brother,
But, she's the one that's in my mind.
She's my love; you're my lover..."

What I am not, I cannot be.
If not my love, Ron, nothing else matters,
For I am looking for the one for me,
To be in his heart, a love and a lover...

Don't Enslave My Soul

"I have many plans," you said.
"Dreams of my heart that were left behind
Because of work, of lack of time,
Marriage, children, responsibilities, and such..."

"I'm looking for nothing else but fun.
To enjoy every moment lost in my past.
I love to dance and dance and dance...
To hold someone close, to embrace her tight..."

"To kiss your lips that's what I like,
To let time swiftly pass us by,
And tenderly hold you
Throughout the night..."

"But, please, don't enslave my soul,
For I don't like to belong to... anyone
That offers me a loving hand.
I like to be free, that's what I like..."

"Please don't talk, don't think.
Don't let me know how you feel for me.
I didn't offer you my heart to give;
I only want to enjoy, to love and live..."

Love Quest

Searching for your lips, a taste of passion from them to drink.
But, although my body was eager to find
A house of love in which to stop,
And close to you, a heart that's mine,
It wasn't there for you to give.
You didn't understand the real "me"...

You never told me about your feelings.
All you talked about was making love,
An empty act with nothing much deeper than touch and "lust"...
I felt so sad, I thought you cared,
But although I searched, my questioning made you mad
Because the loving feeling wasn't there, in your heart...

I was ready to fill
My empty space of only "you,"
But, I found again the lonely "me"
Waiting with extended arms,
And unfulfilled dreams...

And, here I am again... a lonely shadow.
In my soul, a dark and quiet space,
Going toward more empty tomorrows
Until the last and cold embrace of death...

To John

I would like to capture you with my words,
To let you know "me" in just a phrase.
I know, you don't need to say anymore,
Not any more words waste.
"You" just want an instant touch, a fast embrace,
But not my love... I know...

I learned that all you want me for is... lust?...
You came so close to touch my heart,
And stop me with a strange request
From me you want... no love...

You don't want "me," but a tender touch,
A soft kiss, a closed embrace,
From which I should remove my heart?
I can't... I should soon leave,
And soon forget "you" were in my arms...
Soon... John... Goodbye...

Susan Lidia Montes De Aragon

To Bill

*Isn't it funny how destiny waits
To lay a hand and turn our way?...
I was alone and, in my despair,
I met you, but I did not care...*

*I did not care, until you call,
I did not care, until our date.
I knew that because you're a man
You put a show to get your way...*

*But, then, I fill my empty space
With stupid notions that you care,
(I know you don't),
And yet, I'm waiting for your call
To meet again?...*

He

He did not call...
Like a leaf falling into my path
That from a dry, old tree had fall,
He came suddenly into my life...
It was an abrupt awakening of my romantic dreams;
A creeping trembling and unexpected feeling in my heart.
He did not follow or desire my crazy, unfounded wish;
He did not even keep the memory of our meeting in mind.
I know... because he did not call...
He wants to move me away into his past,
Like a little shadow
Of a dove passing in flight.
Because his desire to see me is just a little narrow
Arrow entering, as he desires, into his mind.
I have to erase his deceptive image from my dreams
And to these stupid notions say: GOODBYE!...

Susan Lidia Montes De Aragon

To Peter

Stop playing with my heart.
You toss it—you catch it...
And, with tender affection in your eyes,
You tell me quietly that you love me...
But when night comes along
You forget all about me
And hurriedly to the western dance you go
To hold close all the others.
You asked me if you are the one,
The one that loves me?...
What love are you talking about
If I cannot find it...

Doubts

I cannot erase easily the memories that you left in my mind.
I still cannot believe your sudden goodbye.
I didn't think you could forget so fast
All the moments spent, all the pleasurable instants passed...

My heart aches when I think of you.
I missed the tenderness of your manly hands...
The warm embrace, your adoring kisses,
All the wonderful loving left behind...

But I have to accept we have many problems
(That I, so foolish, like to bury in my mind).
I wanted to ignore them
But I realized that you were right...

Is this enough to endure these obstacles in our lives?...
Do you really love me?...
Or you are planning to take advantage
Of the romantic desires driving my heart?...

Susan Lidia Montes De Aragon

To Peter

In the Valentine card you told me you loved me,
But, when I tenderly looked at your eyes,
You looked away, like if I was bothering,
Interfering with whatever affected your mind.

I slowly moved close to you,
And took softly your hand.
I wanted to stamp a kiss,
And warm up, in loving emotion, your heart...

But you did not look at me
And moved away from my sight.
You ignored me, ignored my attention and affection
When, as a stranger, came back to my side...

What is the reason you want to be with me?...
Companionship is in your mind?...
I don't want a friend or a lover you to be;
I had enough of those in my life...

I know you did not notice:
I'm trying to reach you and touch your heart.
It seems that it's hard for you to know me
Since what I'm offering you cannot find.

Should I continue going
To whatever destiny is drawing in my path?...
I'm just a puppet with a candle burning slowly,
Approaching the end of dying light...

No Connection

I was searching carefully for a sparkle in your eyes
In the emotionless expression of your face.
I was just looking for a sign of love,
A warm gesture to warm my heart...

It was so obvious, there was no connection,
When, next to me, you tried to attract the attention
Of any other attractive lady passing by,
In order to add more to your mental treasures...

And in my presence, it was such a humiliation
To see you adding another woman's number to your collection.
You said you love me,
(It must be another of your mind's inventions)...

What are you looking for
After so many deceptions?...
Another fool that can believe in you,
With no sense of perception?...

You asked me if you are the one I'm searching for,
Are you the man that cares for me (and me alone)?...
Or are you still looking (even when you are with me)
For someone else to come along?...

Susan Lidia Montes De Aragon

Fred

You are here, a good man, with me,
But never romantic enough in all your manners.
My ego, used to manly attention, continuously suffers
When, in your mind, it's not me, but my friend, your ex-
wife, another...

Destiny placed us together, and we have affection.
But, that's not enough, in my dream's expectations,
Because we both have only one crazy desire,
And it drives us both to surrender in passion.

It's not love, lust, or excessive admiration.
We are looking for the warmth in the proximity of our
bodies
As our companion...
Because loneliness brings sadness to our life,
A heart's desolation...

Last night we were miles apart and our passion illusive.
You were not thinking of me when my friend's name
you mentioned.
We have to stop this mismatched union we started,
And continue our search for love, straighten our human
imperfections...

Because this little flame of all our desires
Can go suddenly out and our souls fall forever
In horrible darkness...

To Ron

I found myself with a little time
To think of you, of moments that passed,
To dig within my clouded mind,
And find a light within my heart...

Little I knew of you, except
Of things you said, in casual talk.
Meanwhile you told me "little lies,"
"The same as the other men I met," I thought...

You tried to impress me
Talking about experiences of sexual lust.
Like if the most important treasures
Are the empty pleasures of superficial touch...

You showed me pictures of many women.
You told me of many more.
I didn't care to listen about "past experiences."
My heart listening, closed its doors...

Oh, Ron, what are you looking for?,
One more picture to add to your collection?
Someone to touch in lust and pleasure,
To keep in mind until tomorrow's recollection?...

And, engulfed in deceiving nightly shadows,
Between kisses of passion and tender embraces,
I'm giving in slowly, and your desires followed,
Moved by my own needs for your manly and illusive
protection...

Susan Lidia Montes De Aragon

A Need

There is a need growing in me,
To see you beside me,
Your presence to feel...
As time moves us closer
I experienced your caring.
A growing desire to keep you always,
And I enjoyed the moments,
The tenderness when you caressed
My body so slowly.
I need your embrace to bring me the desired peace
As your love is planting a seed,
And I need to satisfy my thirst for passion
Through the soft touch of your loving lips...
Your soul intertwined with my heart
Is becoming the essence of my being.
What of me if the wind of destiny blows us apart?...

A Trace of You

I needed to fill my empty space
With tender memories of a sweet embrace.
After all, I know you'll soon depart,
And today's loving instance will become another
yesterday...

I know that soon you would be gone,
And I wanted to hold you very close.
To fill my empty cup of love,
To move my heart again
With all the tenderness of your touch,
Before you went away...

I know what you were thinking.
"It was strange
That, when we just were meeting,
 I was giving myself away to you,
Who had, for me, no feelings..."

I wanted you to love me dearly
In just one instance of my life...
To cover me completely with tender kisses,
To drown me an immense sea
Of calm, resting love...

I wanted you to thrill me,
And leave me a trace of you to keep
Because I knew that you were leaving.
The heat of your passion to feel,
And keep it in my mind until future meetings...

Don't Go

Oh, please don't go...
Continue feeding my soul
With flowers that your manly, sweet words
Threw in my path as I passed by you, in my walk.
You had awakened my heart
That lay dormant, sunk in nothingness,
Waiting to feel again alive;
Trembling with emotion,
In eternal hope to light up with love...

Is it too late for me to feel
The tender embrace of a closed one?...
This endless longing for love will never die,
And, among the brittle, dried leaves,
I will be rolling around with the playful wind,
Falling on earth and flying again, free...

Until you have to leave and all my feelings will die,
And I'll put my heart again to sleep,
And in darkness I will fall,
And, again, I will cease to exist...

All About Love

To Howard

You say that, in an instant, you perceived my soul,
Hidden in the many expressions of my mind.
You say that, in a day, you got to understand and know
Some of my love's frustrations, buried secrets in my
life...

From now... where do you like to go?...
Do you wish to enter slowly into my path
To offer me tenderly your hand to walk
Into the chambers of your manly heart?...

Or do you want to be my friend from now on.
Or, in your eyes, am I a lover passing by?...

I have a short road left to travel in this world.
I can only, if you offer, take the flower of your love,
And hold you close as we proceed to go
Through the final pastures, laying in the horizon,
waiting for us...

Susan Lidia Montes De Aragon

The Walk

In a short walk under the stars,
When each one just seems to shine for me;
I heard the wind talk to my heart.
She told me of love, my love for him...

The moon lighted our world.
The stars, each one, gave us a shining smile;
The wind, each night, a song.
You and I gave each other our love...

And with all that belonging to us,
Just take my hand, and close your eyes...

To My Friend from India

Not long ago, I guided myself to your prospective arms,
And, in a short while, in a romantic lapse,
Your lips, unexpectedly, pressed mine,
And my heart felt helpless between your arms...

Each instant lead away by you in a deceitful, delicate manner:
Your face hidden in a chosen night's shadow;
Wanted to see me falling like the soft petals of a young flower
That trapped, without water, look sweet but melted in sorrow...

And suddenly, by surprise, a deceiving feeling
Invaded my whole being, "you" would remain forever in my mind.
You knew, I know, and yet,
Not even that would change your last goodbye...

To Birch

The gentle blow of the wind is touching, moving the leaves.
Above, the sky is extending blue with clouds of cotton,
And every sight of spring of "you" remind me;
Every move and noise set my heart in motion...

At night, the stars just shine to witness
All affairs, from words to tender kisses of lovers.
I reheard empty words and remember again the tender sight,
To look at the moon, the light reflected in your eyes, and wonder...

I wonder, oh Birch, if all is real and true,
If this desire to see you is love.
The tears are fighting to come to my eyes,
And my look is sad, also is my heart...

Sadness

*I cannot stop thinking of you with sadness.
My heart felt helpless when I heard of your feelings.
I opened my heart to all your desires
Because my soul was hoping to stop searching
For the one to love, for the one that loves me...*

*How can you talk of an uncertain ending
To the love relationship we're having?...
(You that "desire, love and missed me
Because of obligations with my family?")*

*I cannot get used to the idea that I will not see you anymore.
My heart is aching continuously
When I think that every feeling of my love for you I'll have to abort...
It's an eternal battle when my mind says: "You must..."
And my soul wishes to hold on...*

Susan Lidia Montes De Aragon

Another Plan

I welcomed you into my arms
To soothe the pain caused by a broken, past love.
I liked your eyes, your warm smile,
Your gentle hands that touched my heart...

And I was feeling very close
To tell you secrets and open doors,
Because more valuable than gold
Is the gift of mind and soul...

I was waiting to nourish my life
With you each day a little more,
To read the light within your eyes
To slowly move you very close...

But destiny had another plan prepared,
And ignoring my inquisitive words,
You opened your hand and dropped my heart,
Walked away and never called...

The Man Doesn't Love Me

The man doesn't love me.
Why do I persist nourishing a feeling
That has no echo in the chambers of his heart?...
Just because my soul cannot be living
Without the warm torch of a tender romance...

He doesn't love me.
He doesn't stay with me but just passes by.
He doesn't hold me next to him,
Or explore my face, or meet my eyes...

He doesn't love me... and
Even though my empty heart is eager to love,
I could not touch his soul with all my kisses
Nor guide his steps toward my loving side...

He doesn't know or care about my wishes.
He wants to feel free to all to love...
I should not waste his time or mine just thinking,
I'll set him free, and say "goodbye"...

Susan Lidia Montes De Aragon

Do I Look Like Her?...

What are you looking for?...
A shadow passing through my being
That you desire to bring forth
Because you like to bring her back in me?...
(The one you love and you have lost)...

Do I look like her?...
Maybe in an instant short.
Does my smile inspire to be,
Deep in your heart, the hope
That you secretly seek?...

Look deep into my eyes and into my soul.
I'm not her... I'm me...
And if you desire my love,
See if I'm the one you wish...

Because I'm also looking for someone closed
To offer me the tenderness I need
Until the wind of winter the pages of my life will close,
And I will be ready for the restful peace...

To Howard

We parted calmly,
Like if we never met before;
Like if our long, passional romance
Was only a futile dream
That came and soon was gone
In a profound dream we had.

You saw me every day,
And I wanted you to love me with all your heart,
But I could not cheer up the sad expression of your face
Nor see the sparkle of love deep in your eyes.

We both the end expected,
It was no surprise when we became apart,
As we suspected.
And my soul is bleeding with melancholic sadness
In a careless world that moves us,
Back and forth, in all its madness...

Our minds did not meet anymore,
Like if all the memories,
Like the leaves, were blown
By the cold wind of winter,
To freeze all tender feelings we had before.
(How can such a profound feeling to nothingness fall?...)

To Mr. Goodman

I did not know when I met you
That you would share my heart;
It was a cruel awakening, a sudden surprise,
To end soon in a sad goodbye...
I felt your eyes looked at my soul,
And only loving dreams came to my mind.
I did not know you would close the doors
Before you allowed our courtship to start.
You were so afraid to trust again
And surrender to a new love,
Because you did not like me in a day
You shut your ears and pushed away my heart.
You told me: "Goodbye"
"Not interested in you..." you said,
And pushed my dreams of love aside...

Poor Heart

Poor heart of mine,
Eager to love.
Embracing only the empty space
Of someone that could of being,
But it's not there.
Looking deep into your soul,
To find an echo to any tender jest,
To find an inch of love
In the cold expression of your face...
To stop to rest in the warm protection
Of your tight embrace.
How illusive was all the passion
That led me, adoring you, to your bed.
My arms, extended, found only emptiness,
And my heart, lonely and sad,
Is still searching...

Terry

Searching for your lips,
A drink of passion from them to drink.
But, although my body was eager to find
A house of love in which to stop,
And, closed to you, a heart that's mine,
It wasn't there for you to give.

You never told me about your feelings.
All you talked about was making love,
An empty act with nothing much deeper
Than touch and lust...

I felt so sad,
I thought you did care, but although I searched,
My questioning made you mad
Because the loving feeling wasn't there,
In your heart...

Terry: I was ready to fill
My empty space of only you.
But, I found again the lonely me,
Waiting with extended arms,
And unfulfilled dreams of love.

And, here I am again... a lonely shadow.
In my soul, a dark and quiet space,
Going toward more empty tomorrows
Until the last, cold embrace of death...

Frustration

I could not find the arms to run in sorrow and despair;
I could not find anyone to understand,
And my spiritual treasures to embrace.
No one that, when I needed love,
A hug and kiss would spare.
And now only frustration I feel, anger no more,
For all my beginnings in this ending I lost...

Susan Lidia Montes De Aragon

Without Love

My heart is yearning to feel your warmth,
But, although my arms, extended, are waiting for your embrace,
You are not responding, you are still silent and cold,
In a corner, working, active in your important life,
And ignoring my soul, that is passing you by...
How long do you think this passion can endure
Without feeding my life with the love that my soul lights?...
You have to know that for me,
Without love, this passion will die...

The Quiet Look

I extended my arms to find the warmth
I'm longing from your heart,
And puzzled, I found a negative response.
Your arms laid calmly at your body's side...

My figure drop dead in the endless night,
And suddenly, faded into a lonely shadow...
I looked at you...my eyes eager to find
A sign of love in your quiet look, that followed...

Susan Lidia Montes De Aragon

To Eddie

*Because it's been
30 days or more,
I'll wait for you,
For your hello...*

*And with every "bye," I wondered
Will you remember anymore?...
And for 30 days, I'll wait
Next to the phone...*

*And, when we meet,
Your face of happiness seems to glow.
We dance and dance until we fall,
And, in the middle of it all,
We hide in shadows of the night
To hold each other very close.
All night, all night until the dawn
You share with me your body's warmth.
But, then, it's time to say "goodbye,"
And that, that is all...*

*My brief companion of the night,
I need you so...
With every embrace that you give me,
You embrace my soul...*

*What are you?...
Friend... or lover... or...?*

Goodbye!

They told me that you don't care for me,
And I felt a heavy hand of sadness fall in my heart...
My mind, cluttered with doubts, did not want to believe
That the same lips that told me "I love you" were
planning to murmur "goodbye"...

How can your hands, that caressed me so tenderly,
Push me away from your adoring side?...
What happened to your tender kisses,
To your warm embraces, that nurtured my soul every
night?...

I feel an agonizing pain, like a dagger
Piercing my heart as I look at your smile.
How can you tell me that you love me
When there is a plan to forget me in your mind?...

How can you betray my trust after you inspired what I
feel?...
Let's depart from each other now.
Don't say anymore... enough pain I carry as I leave.
Goodbye... my love...

Goodbye feelings, goodbye hope, goodbye to all loving
thoughts
Of an imagined future, that died.
Dried leaves that keep rolling away
From this old tree, my life...

Michael

You finally called, we finally met.
Tender words, kisses, a soft touch.
Loving encounters that nourished my soul,
And time slowly passed by.
All I needed is a shoulder to rest,
Your arms to relax...

I absorbed and wished the delight to prolong
For tomorrow, and tomorrows until the last of my breaths.
To lift me, and move me to a soft cloud beyond,
To enclose me in your arms
Away from this world.
Someone to hold me when life is too hard...

And now that you're gone,
Just the longing of that loving feeling
Lingers in my mind,
With a painful desire
To relive your love in my heart...

Eddie

Time passes by
And years come and go...
Like leaves in plants
That always grow,
And dries, and change
Green into gold,
They're here now,
Tomorrow gone...

Time passes by.
It's just like love
When it is born
And never nurtured,
It's like a little candlelight,
Going out until it's gone.
But, Eddie, when love is given warmth,
It lingers in our heart
And grows each day a little more...

You lighted the candle with your hello
But only once, and once alone.
In silent nights, your body talks,
And with your departure, it slowly goes...
And, for 30 days, you don't even try
To write, to listen, or get in touch.
I wait, wondering, if after 30 days,
The warmth, the feeling, still survives...

No... I need you more
Than just a passing moment in my life.
I missed you for 30 days,
Before you call me to meet my path.
Eddie, unless you try,
It will be lost,
And, in my heart, your love be gone.
It will get cold, it will get cold...

Susan Lidia Montes De Aragon

Pure Delight

As I close my eyes to put my mind to rest,
A warm glimpse of your manly face
Still lingers in there,
And comes to nourish my lonely heart...

As you kissed with your lips my cheek,
Very close to surrender to you I was.
I needed to hear again those manly words, adoring lies,
That brings forgotten feelings, buried in my heart,
alive...

Let me relive again my secret wish,
Fall in a bath of pure delight.
Take me to Heaven with a tender kiss
Before I go to sleep and let my dreams forever die...

All About Love

I Should of Known

Why continue searching for a door to our heart in vain,
If you are not feeling tenderness for me?...
I have to only mitigate this profound pain
That your indifference to my heart caused me to feel...

I should of suspected it
When your eyes avoided meeting mine.
When your arms laid still on your side
Trying to keep me distant from your touch...

I should of known
When my lips searching for yours,
Did not find warmth
But an empty and probable goodbye.

And let the passing time, the future days,
Bring me the perfect love in which I finally will rest.
Maybe I should accept my destiny;
Make loneliness my friend...

Probably the love of God
Should be my only love
As I approach my end.

Susan Lidia Montes De Aragon

Ring of Fire

Here I am, with my chest naked...
With my lips untouched, pale, frozen...
Waiting to fill my soul, that is still empty,
To resuscitate dreams, that passed, fell, broken...

Where is the love I hope for, to stay forever?
The warmth of a heart, the arms to hold me,
The chest where I lean my head to rest,
Meanwhile, fingers of love tenderly touch my forehead...

And here you were, at my side,
To look at me for a moment...
Your heart floating in the mist of life,
Looking busy, creative, wild, but lonely...
In a musical background of notes,
In which, I passed by, and you ignored me...

Meanwhile our souls keep floating,
Your lips knew the words to fill a woman's heart
With false, romantic dreams,
That, probably, will be broken...

My hands touched your hands
In a kind gesture of tenderness.
Your lips caressed me and threw me in a ring of passion,
To which I fell, in a peaceful surrender...

And, I'm in a bed of soft clouds
That, momentarily, is taking me to Heaven;
In which my thoughts, which keep me weary,
Could be, forever, buried...

I cannot help wondering where this path of fire will
finally take me.
I am in a pleasurable ring of fire,
Which flames can suddenly be blown off
By the playful wind that is passing...

All About Love

The Last Word

Engulfed in the darkness of the night,
Falling slowly in a welcomed restful trance,
It was so delightful to invite you to my mind
(Feeling the protective embrace of your manly arms,
Still around me when you were gone.)
Like a warm flame still lighting with happiness my
heart...

And then, came the days of lovers: Valentine.
I felt your love when I slowly read your card.
I enjoyed the close embrace during the night,
The tender touch of your hands moving slowly,
Invading my soul with the wonderful pleasure of your
magic touch...
You, my dear lover, the only man I wanted to love...

Today, you chose to leave me
Because I could not feel the passion of your love,
And other reasons of incompatibility troubling your
mind.
Because, when we were together,
There were words that we carelessly let slip from our
mouths,
And stayed engraved, hurting our egos, punching our
prides.

It's so hard to bury this feeling
That yesterday filled with dreams my heart.
(I still wanted to climb a mountain
To save this dying love...)

But you felt helpless
And wanted to remove me completely from your mind,
Bury deep any affection inspired by my touch,
And you chose to say "goodbye..."

Susan Lidia Montes De Aragon

*I felt an unexpected pain bursting my heart,
And my eyes freed the sad tears that again would darken my life.
Yesterday, a love that filled me with dreams,
Today, the love that has to die...*

Goodbye friend... goodbye lover... goodbye love...

Betrayal

Your image came coming back, and back,
Appearing constantly between the shadows of the night,
Keeping me from resting,
Breaking the calm beating of my heart...

Please painful agony, go away!...
Accept his horrible betrayal of my love.
And finally have the strength to pull the knife
He plunged into my heart that dreadful night
I heard him talking to the other one...

He preferred to leave me, lonely, once again.
After he managed to intrude into my life,
And left me with my arms extended,
Only embracing the cold space
With no one else by my side...

The morning light will erase
From my tortured mind
Every trace of how he threw away
The key to let him in into my heart,
And broke in pieces the dreams
He awoke again to brighten my path.

Please let these sad and painful tears he caused
Wash away forever this horrible burning of his love,
Until it finally dies and disappears within my soul...

Susan Lidia Montes De Aragon

Don't Talk to Me

I know that although your heart is searching
There's no spark in your heart for me,
And, in the quest of the love for which my soul is yearning,
I'm still resisting to accept that we cannot be.

I asked you, last night, if you wish my love forever,
And you answered, in a quiet tone of voice, "As you wish…"
How can a man that says he waits impatiently
To hold me in his arms in togetherness,
Respond with an emotionless "Maybe"?

Don't talk to me again in romantic phrases,
Let my soul in quiet peace once more.
Only when you welcome my love and return it
Will be when, in tender murmur, I'll be ready to listen your adoring words.

In the Cold

And when the night is coming sweet,
To think of you is only a dream,
That fills my heart with wonderful hope
To find you again in a turning point
Of life, now here, tomorrow gone...
You turned the light in my lonely
Dark soul,
And, when you left,
You turned it off
To leave me standing
In the cold...

Puzzled

I met you not knowing
If I was going to find deep in your soul
The offer of love to sweeten my heart,
The welcomed peace I'm looking for...

And you gave me:
The tenderness of a sweet embrace.
I let myself be engulfed
In a bubble of passion, and in delight fell...

But, although I searched,
I could not find a spark of love in your eyes
Or a soft look in your manly face...
I felt uneasy at your side

When, just like any other man, your attention was taken
By another attractive woman passing by,
And, ignoring my presence,
You were indifferent to my broken pride...

I could no longer pretend that you loved me,
You would remain like an unsolved puzzle,
Lingering in my mind,
Until I finally decided to said "Goodbye"...

Lust

I try to find a moment's peace
In the turmoil of life, to meditate...
To grasp an inch of sanity
Before I lose it all, to escape
Into the peaceful, quiet chambers of my soul
To save my mind before it's late...

And you came into my sight...
Your gentle, manly manners
Embraced my lonely heart,
Caressed my soul, calmed down my mind...

I welcomed every moment,
Enjoyed every pastime that we had.
I believed in your affection,
And slowly surrendered into your loving arms...

And in the beautiful warmth of your embrace,
Showered with the tenderness of your loving touch,
We loved each other
Into the late hours of the night...

Until your words put a stop to the feelings of my heart;
The truth brought reality to my childish mind:
You're just a man, like any other man,
And in your manly mind: an insignificant wish for "lust"...

Susan Lidia Montes De Aragon

Why?...

I don't understand what drives my mind
To think of you...
You certainly did not try
To tell me pretty words and move
My heart...
You even told me:
You want adventure... but not romance...
Then, why did I think of you?
If you are putting always aside
All feelings that for me are good...
You want, with me, a friendship that will last,
A friend more, in my large group,
And I don't mind...
But... my heart is moved
For being ignored, as you passed by,
And calmly smile throwing a look
That is engraved deep in my mind.
And returns to delight me in my dreams...
Until I wake... and realize
There is no reason for what I feel:
In you "love" I will not find,
"Romance" is not your wish,
And I have to turn this page in the journey of my life...

All About Love

To Fernando

You touched my lips,
And with your strong arms
My body surrounded.
It was easy for me
To fall like a broken flower.
There was magic in your touch,
Although I knew it was loveless.
There was no tenderness
But a feverish madness
That drove us both,
Hidden among the shadows of the night.
Trying to find warmth under the covers.
You told me sweet words
That only lovers uttered.
I tried not to believe them
So my heart, later, will not suffer,
But, oh, foolish heart.
You invited, again, the butterflies into my garden,
And, when you left, ignoring me,
You took my last hope to satisfy my deep desires...

Susan Lidia Montes De Aragon

Planting a Seed

There is a need growing in me:
To see you beside me,
Your presence to feel...
As time moves us closer,
I experience your caring,
A growing desire to keep you always...
I enjoyed the moments,
The tenderness when you caress
My body so slowly...
I need your embrace to bring me the desired peace.
Your love is planting a seed...
And I need to quench my thirst for passion
Through a soft touch of your loving lips.
You are becoming part of me;
Your soul intertwined with my heart
Is becoming the essence of my being...

He Doesn't Care for Me

He doesn't care for me, I know...
He only wants to spread his wings
And fly away, his freedom holds
The peace of mind he wants to achieve...
For I was told, he doesn't care for me,
I know...

He wants to hold my body closed
And steal the passion I can give.
He wants my body and leaves my soul
Abandoned, lonely, without the affection that it needs...
He doesn't care for me,
I know...

And then, if nothing he can feel,
Let him depart, to others take the road.
Without love my heart cannot persist
Lighting the passion that my body holds...

Susan Lidia Montes De Aragon

To Larry

I closed my eyes and let myself go,
My heart so lonely was eager to find the warmth
In the closed embrace of the man
Who just passed me by, but in my mind, stayed, enclosed,
With an anxious desire that he'll be able
To awake my heart with loving joy...

And I let myself go,
And, in a childish game
I let him know
Of my innermost desires to hold him close...

And we lay holding each other.
To my surprise, our passion rapidly unfolds.
And, closing my eyes to reason,
I unleash all the fire that hides in my soul,
And my body followed in a quick response...

I was pleased to meet him
I wanted to know him, each day, more and more.
But, to my surprise, he told me he had another,
And my heart, in pain, closed again its door...

All About Love

To Michael

In the turmoil of my life,
Searching for peace, a moment's rest,
Many souls, parading, crossed my path,
But, I stopped a moment with you, to stay,
And you offered the sparkle of your smile,
The closeness and warmth of your embrace...
You traced pictures of all your future plans
Empty pages to be filled, old ones to erase.
These are your tomorrow dreams,
Some, sad nightmares to forget...
You want me falling into your passion,
Trapped, like flies in a spider web.
But, did you forget the bleeding of my heart
Because I will not hear your tender words, someday?...
What is hidden within the corner of your heart?...
Are you really the man
To offer me the profound, true offering of your love?
Or will you leave, the hands of fate to move you away...

To Jack

I'm digging down into the corners of my mind
To find out why I let you in,
Into the fibers of my heart;
And I continuously tried and persisted.
Although I felt you distant all the time...

Your thoughts were all for her.
(I saw it deep into your eyes)...
You secretly love her so.
Her name engraved into your heart...

Stubborn I, I still have hope.
And, like a fool,
I gave you me!... I gave you ALL!...
(Nobody to blame... It was my fault...)

Now I can't stop the incessant pain in my heart
Since your last words to me, your last goodbye.
And, with the thought of you stamp in my life,
I'm going to be alone for a long while...

(Or until another pass me by...)

All About Love

(To all my friends...)
Sparks of Dreams That Have Not Died

Come... come see into my eyes,
Inside them, those lights,
Sparks of dreams that have not die;
And, although years have passed me by,
The well of love have not yet dried
And hope to find it again drives on my life...

Come... come see into my eyes,
Can you perceive in them
A melancholic sight?
All the loneliness that a smile
Cannot hide.
And, far, a sight can only catch
The invisible one that loves ME
And I cannot find...

And, all there are,
Are men that like to hold my hand;
Dancing around, around,
Are actors, puppets, imitators
That act like if they are in love
But wish to hide from me their hearts...

Susan Lidia Montes De Aragon

To Peter

Why do I come to you?... Don't you know?...
Every sweet moment that we both enjoy
It's nourishment for my poor soul
Hungry for love
So just close your eyes, let's not talk,
All I want to do is just to absorb
The tenderness you show me tonight.
And then I'll put to sleep,
Floating in dreams, my heart.
And yearning for more and more and more,
I'll wait for the next morning light to come.
Until your arms can hold me again all night long...

Sam

"Here comes Sam, there's the man," I said,
I talked and talked, and laughed with him,
And slowly on his shoulder leaned my head.
Oh yes, I talked and listened to his words,
And through it all, absorbed the strength
That only HE had brought to me, my FRIEND...

Here comes Sam, HE's the man,
Who is so different, he is thoughtful, profound and understanding,
NOT LIKE THE REST.
Oh, YES, HE's the one I trust, my friend...

And in one instant of a night,
I closed my eyes, and said, "Oh YES,
I like to leave my FRIEND behind
To meet the Sam I thought a MAN"...

And lead by passion, hand in hand,
Engulfed in shadows of the night,
I looked at him, with tender thoughts of love,
And took his hands, giving in, to all manly desires of his mind...

And then, I looked at him,
Expecting care, affection to find,
And eager said "Here is my heart, you like to have?"...
"No", he said, "Please leave... Goodbye!..."

Susan Lidia Montes De Aragon

Your Charming Smile

How can I resist your charming smile
From penetrating into the chambers of my heart.
To fall, like in a hypnotic trance,
In a beautiful garden of pure delight...
Your face with those manly, boyish eyes,
The way you moved when I'm around;
The tender softness of your touch
That oh, so affectionate, can only bring a spark
To awake my dreams, dormant in a romantic past...

Please don't be sad;
I know the secret that hides in your mind:
The only love that you love and love so much
Have thrown you away from her adoring side...
What can you do? In your useless fight
But surrender into the destiny awaiting in your path.
I know... I'm only here a moment's time,
Like a handkerchief for your sorrow to wipe...

You only want my warm embrace
To help you stand the pain and help you by.
When, oh so lonely, it's easy to fall in a trap,
Like a little insect in her flight,
To get a false but wonderful illusion
When you starve for love...

Prayer for Love

When my heart touches the pillow every night,
I pray earnestly to my dear God;
To slow back for me the clock of everlasting time,
Until, he let me meet the love of mine...
Please hold the hands of my life
From marking my face,
Because of the lashes of suffering that have passed...
Stop sickening my body
From all the hard work that I have done...
Because, before I'm gone,
And the last beat of my heart slows down,
I like the hands of my tender love
To touch...
I cannot stand the thought
Of lonely, empty nights,
Without the warmth of the embrace I need so much...
Let me kiss the lips of my only one
Before the kiss of death
Blows away the flame of life...

Susan Lidia Montes De Aragon

Hi Emptiness

I was still feeling your heart warming my heart,
The pressure of your arms in your embrace,
The tender memory of the night you made love to me
Before you left...

It's hard to grasp that all THAT
Was the imagination of my mind in all its crave
For an instant moment of love
That wasn't there...

So, as you wish,
Goodbye my love,
Hi emptiness...

A Tender Moment

I let myself be led
To fall helplessly into your arms;
My soul in a bath of passion to be wet
And lost in a dream of love I was;
Because you hold me in your sweet embrace.
Let me grasp in an instant breath
The tender moment you bring to me.
It's only my lonely heart
That holds, in secret, an anxious wish
To take capture your manly heart
And be lost in a Paradise of Love
Until the final, eternal sleep of night

Because, I know
That, next, to come,
Was the end of it all.
An unexpected, and last goodbye.

Susan Lidia Montes De Aragon

Without Love

I'm still waiting for the one to awake my heart
From this dreamless sleep...
Because when in his arms he'll enclose my heart
Finally I'll feel protected and my life complete...

There a short road left of my journey.
Is it too late for me to hope for love?...
Is it waiting for me someday?... or is it over...
Should my arms still be extended for someone to come?...

And within my heart, there's only emptiness,
A big spot waiting to be filled with warm affection,
And a desperate anguish of loneliness
That only a kiss can quiet or... my secret hope of expectations...

Nobody can live without love
And hoping it, we create dreams,
That moves us forward to survive
And gives meaning to our soul to exist...

Because without love, there is no life...

All About Love

To Charles

I know that soon you would be gone
And I wanted to hold you very close...

To fill my empty cup of love,
To move my heart again
With all the tenderness of your touch
Before you went away...

I know what you were thinking;
It was strange
That, when we just were meeting
I was giving myself to you,
Who had, for me, no feeling...

I wanted you to love me dearly
In just one instant of my life.
To cover me completely with tender kisses,
To drown me in an immense sea of calm, resting love...

I wanted you to thrill me,
And leave me a trace of you to keep.
Because, I knew that you were leaving.
And I wanted the ecstasy of your passion to feel
And keep it in my mind until future meetings...

I needed you to fill my empty space
With tender memories of a sweet embrace.
After all, I knew you'll soon depart
And today's loving instant will become another of my
yesterdays...

Susan Lidia Montes De Aragon

Fade Away...

For a few moments I thought I could re-live
The love that filled my heart with joy.
But now, the chance is gone.
Only a few instances left in my short life,
That is running faster than the filtered
Grains of sand that thru my fingers fall...
And years are passing by,
Taking away the youth that held my body fresh and strong...
All those dreams deep in my heart,
That never came to be, are going to be bury
With my body, and my soul...
Maybe, someday, the sun will wake again
The being that, dormant in the land, has gone to sleep
Before all her desires eternally fade away...

All About Love

Thanks!...

Engulfed in the delight of a passionate heart,
I was bathed with happy illusions of a long, awaiting love...
"You" offered me your loving lips,
Your hands, like feathers, caressing me...

I left your side, a little kiss, a little hug,
A sweet smile, and then... a bye!...

To "You" that kiss me tenderly,
Embrace me warmly...
To those that came to my life, and have to depart...
To "You" that loved me, and "Those" that loved me not...

Thanks for the sweet drinks to warm me up,
And the "Remembrances" in future dark and lonely nights...

All About Love

To My One and Only

*Because with your warmth and kindness
You vanished the sadness and calmed the anguish
of my heart,
To fill my mind with tender thoughts of love
And bring a smile to my face and life...*

www.ingramcontent.com/pod-product-compliance
Lightning Source LLC
Chambersburg PA
CBHW020017050426
42450CB00005B/511